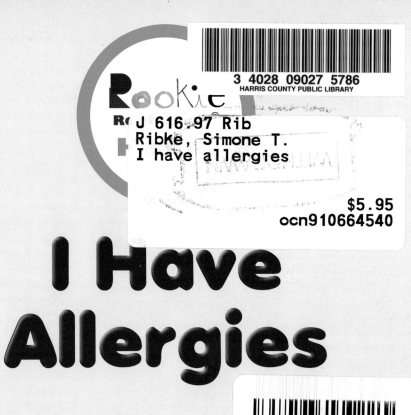

I Have Allergies

by Simone T. Ribke

Content Consultant
Catherine A. Dennis, N.P.

Reading Consultant
Jeanne M. Clidas, Ph.D.
Reading Specialist

Children's Press®
An Imprint of Scholastic Inc.

Library of Congress Cataloging-in-Publication Data
Ribke, Simone T., author.
I have allergies/by Simone T. Ribke.
    pages cm. — (Rookie read about health)
Summary: "Introduces the reader to allergies" — Provided by publisher.
Includes index.
ISBN 978-0-531-22704-6 (library binding) — ISBN 978-0-531-22580-6 (pbk.)
    1. Allergy—Juvenile literature. 2. Immune system—Juvenile literature. I. Title.
II. Series: Rookie read-about health.
RC584.R52 2016
    616.97—dc23   2015021122

Produced by Spooky Cheetah Press
Design by Keith Plechaty

Printed in China 62

SCHOLASTIC, CHILDREN'S PRESS, ROOKIE READ-ABOUT®, and associated logos are trademarks and/or registered trademarks of Scholastic Inc.

1 2 3 4 5 6 7 8 9 10 R 25 24 23 22 21 20 19 18 17 16

Table of Contents

Why So Sneezy?

Are your eyes itchy and watery in spring? Does your nose get stuffy and sneezy? Is there any food you cannot eat? Is there any medicine you cannot take? If so, you may have an allergy.

Do not worry. If you have an allergy, you are not alone. Fifty million Americans have allergies. That is almost one in every six people!

Pollen floating through the air can cause allergies.

This illustration shows immune cells attacking germs (in green).

How Your Body Works

You have an **immune system.**
It attacks germs that enter your
body. It helps you stay healthy.
Sometimes the immune system
cannot kill the germs. That is when
you get sick. When this happens,
you will have **symptoms**, such as
a fever. That shows your immune
system is working.

Things other than germs
enter our bodies every day.
We breathe in things from the air.
We eat different foods. We touch
lots of things. Sometimes the
immune system makes a mistake.
It thinks something harmless is
harmful. Its response is called
an allergy.

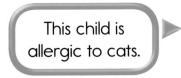

This child is
allergic to cats.

Types of Allergies

Many people are allergic to something they breathe in from the air. This can include pollen and **dust mites**. It can also include pet dander. Pet dander is little flakes of an animal's skin.

This girl is allergic to pollen.

Some people are allergic to certain foods. Food allergies can be very bad. Some cause anaphylactic (a-nuh-fuh-LAK-tik) shock. That is when a person's mouth and throat swell up.
He or she has trouble breathing.
This is very dangerous.
Medical help is needed right away!

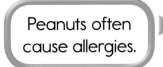

Peanuts often cause allergies.

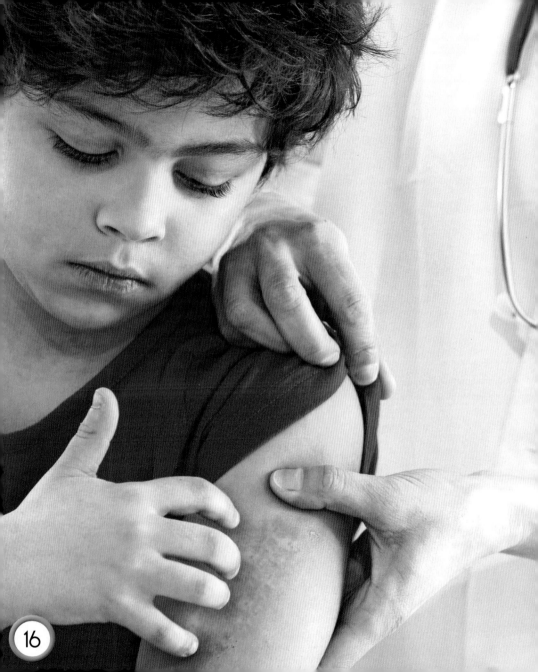

Some people are allergic to certain medicines. These allergies can cause hives. Hives are red patches on the skin.

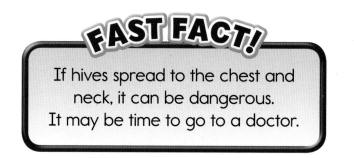

FAST FACT!

If hives spread to the chest and neck, it can be dangerous. It may be time to go to a doctor.

Another type of severe allergy is to insect bites or stings. Insects such as bees, wasps, hornets, and yellow jackets inject **venom** when they sting. Fire ants inject venom when they bite. For some people, this can cause anaphylactic shock.

This is a photo of a bee stinging someone. ▶

Some people have skin allergies. They are allergic to something they touch. For example, some people are allergic to soap, grass, or latex. Doctors' gloves are usually made of latex. Skin allergies usually cause a rash.

For people with a latex allergy, a doctor needs to use plastic gloves.

What Can You Do?

People with allergies have to stay away from the things that cause them. For example, people with a peanut allergy may have to eat lunch at a peanut-free table. They may even have to bring their own food to parties.

Sometimes there is a sign (inset) showing that a lunch table is peanut-free.

Peanut- and
Nut-Free Table

Please Wash Hands

People with allergies can also take an antihistamine (an-tie-HISS-tuh-meen). This medicine helps fight allergic reactions. It can make allergy sufferers feel better.

FAST FACT!

Some antihistamines can make you sleepy.

People with severe allergies need to carry an EpiPen at all times. This is not really a pen. It is a shot. An EpiPen stops anaphylactic shock. It injects medicine into the body. It keeps the person safe until he or she gets to the hospital for treatment.

So even when you are itchy and sneezy, do not worry. There are ways you can feel better!

Some kids wear a bracelet to let others know they have severe allergies.

Use EPI-pen in EMERG

Your Turn

Take this quiz to see how much you have learned about allergies.

1. Sneezing can be a sign of an allergy. **True or False?**

2. An EpiPen is great for drawing. **True or False?**

3. Antihistamines can help you feel better if you have allergies. **True or False?**

Answers: 1. true; 2. false; 3. true

Allergy Smarts

Which one of these is *not* a symptom of an allergy?

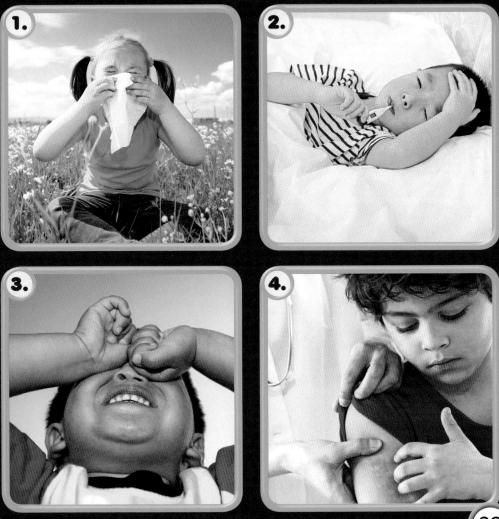

1.

2.

3.

4.

Answer: 2

Strange but True!

Some people eat local honey to help outdoor allergies. Local honey is made nearby. Bees collect nectar from flowers to make honey. They collect pollen at the same time. When you eat the honey, you eat small amounts of pollen. This may help your body get used to the pollen. In time, you may be less allergic to the pollen.

Just for Fun

Q: What does a train with an allergy sound like?

A: Ah-choo-choo-choo!

Q: How can you keep your nose from running?

A: Take away its sneakers!

Glossary

dust mites (dust MIGHTS): tiny bugs that live on dust

immune system (ih-MYOON SIS-tum): system that protects the body against disease and infection

symptoms (SIMP-tums): changes in the body that are signs of an illness

venom (VEH-num) poison produced by some insects, snakes, and spiders

Index

Facts for Now

Visit this Scholastic Web site for more information on allergies:
www.factsfornow.scholastic.com
Enter the keyword **Allergies**

About the Author

Simone T. Ribke writes children's books, and she is also an artist.
Simone lives with her husband, children, and schnauzer in Maryland.
She is allergic to dust mites and rhubarb.